In the Dreaming

In the Dreaming

Selected Poems

William Dickey

The University of Arkansas Press
Fayetteville   1994

Library of Congress Cataloging-in-Publication Data

Dickey, William.
    In the dreaming : selected poems / William Dickey.
        p.   cm
    ISBN 1-55728-285-4 (cloth). — ISBN 1-55728-286-2 (paper)
    I. Title
    PS3507.I28I4   1993
    811'.54—dc20
                                            93-1098
                                              CIP

For Len & Merlin & Sylvia

Acknowledgments

Poems in this collection originally appeared in *Aisling, The Atlantic Monthly, Big Moon, Blue Unicorn, Bottomfish, Carleton Miscellany, The Carolina Quarterly, The Cutting Edge, The Georgia Review, Hudson Review, The International Portland Review, Kansas Quarterly, Massachusetts Review, New England Review/Bread Loaf Quarterly, New Letters, New World Writing, The New Yorker, Poetry Now, Poetry*Texas, Quanta, Western Review,* and *The Yale Review.* I am grateful to the editors of these publications for their encouragement, and for their permission to reprint the poems.

Poems here have also been included in previous collections of my poetry: *Brief Lives* (The Heyeck Press); *Interpreter's House* (Ohio State University Press); *Joy* (Pterodactyl Press); *The King of the Golden River* (Pterodactyl Press); *More under Saturn* (Wesleyan University Press); *Of the Festivity* (Yale University Press); *The Rainbow Grocery* (University of Massachusetts Press); *The Sacrifice Consenting* (Pterodactyl Press). *Of the Festivity* was included in the Yale Series of Younger Poets; *The Rainbow Grocery* received the Juniper Prize from the University of Massachusetts Press.

The work included here has been supported, over the years, by Fulbright and Woodrow Wilson fellowships, by grants from the American Academy and Institute of Arts and Letters and the National Endowment for the Arts, and by sabbatical leaves granted by San Francisco State University, and I am truly appreciative of this assistance.

Contents

III.   Gambling at Reno

I

Love among
the Manichees

The Dolls Play at Hansel and Gretel

1.

They hunch their heads against the fable of night,
their thin wax heads with eyes that are too large;
each one examines the bruises of the day.

When they are through with this they take their parts:
this one is witch, and this one is the wood,
trees flit into his huddled brain, and owls.

And the poor children, the senseless, shabby things,
cluttered with pebbles that will do no good,
lift their rag hands and imitate despair:

"Why have you put us out into the cold:
all day, helpless as any human child,
we have been yours to fondle or destroy,

you made us saints or thieves or prostitutes,
you put us slyly in Jocasta's bed;
mother and father, what we are is yours,

we fought the wars you could not fight alone,
but at the end of the garden you said go,
and we sprawled nameless in the pitying flowers.

Now in the dark the Doppelgänger winks
to say the path goes on as it always has.
Bushes take foot, and the wood closes in."

2. The Witch's Song

In the epileptic fit
when your bones were scarcely knit
you beheld the paradise
of my parti-colored eyes.

In the foul delirium
when the cockatrices come,
eager to delay the truth
you have kissed my withered mouth.

Now let hand release its hold
on the world you have been told,
let the sleeping eyelid fall
shutting out the sight of all.

Coiling in the middle ear,
let my word be what you hear,
let my hand that sews and clips
snip your tongue and stitch your lips.

In my body you will find
mathematics of the blind,
malformations there and scars
of the potent integers.

In the crevice of my gown
secret lies your mortal town,
in the science of my breast
is your formula of rest.

3. The Gingerbread House's Song

Wind the thread and wind the thread,
mother married with a sailor,
and I thought that I was dead
if her common sense could fail her.
But I buttoned up my fright
and I strangled him at night.

Turn the spool and turn the spool,
father took a witch for daughter.
Then I knew he was a fool—
witches can't cross running water.
Like an angel in a dream
I immersed her in the stream.

Sing the song and sing the song,
all the nightingales are hidden.
Right is right and wrong is wrong,
folk must do what they are bidden
or I take them by the neck
and I put them in my sack.

Cast the stone and cast the stone,
eat the muscle and the marrow,
eat the body to the bone.
It will rise again tomorrow
worshiping the hand that slew,
and had every right to do.

Close the eye and close the eye,
all things come to him that wishes.

Now the world is only I
I am finding it delicious.
Powerful, virile, handsome, young,
I taste the blood upon my tongue.

4. The Oven's Song

The toad
glitters in the night
from the jewel in its head.
Everything else is dead.
I did not bring you.
I will not take you.
Fancies of lunacy glitter in your head.

Only the same door
from the same room and into the same room.
Under this time
it is the same time that it was before
when you came and will come.
Circle the stone with marks to mark your time.
You will remember nothing of them here.

Only the box,
and the locks,
and the nail.
You are unwounded yet, but you will fail.
As soon as you start to know, the wounds will come,
blood in the pricked thumb,

blood on the shirt,
till all of you is drained and put aside,
folded like paper on a shelf.

You are yourself.
Cuddle into my entrail and be still.
There is no tie between you and my will,
but an indifference.
What you hear
runs on as steady in my ear
as the noise made by an indifferent machine.
I will not say what you have been,

that is concern, and I am not concerned.
I am the toad's jewel at the center of the skull.
I am what you have earned.

5.

Their thin wax heads are scattered on the grass,
their button eyes look dully at the sky
where it has begun to rain. The morning comes.

Empty and destitute, they disarrange
the order of life, until the children come
telling them what are their identities.

Memoranda

The scars take us back to places we have been,
cities named Masochism or Inaccuracy.
This little one between the finger and the thumb
is something that my brother did to me
on a hot Washington's Birthday in the past,
when we were young and cruelly competent;
In a miniature world like a glass fishing float
he was the total image of intent.

Who stuck the pencil point into my palm?
It is so long ago that I cannot say,
but the black stick of graphite under the skin—
some friend, some enemy put it there that way
to succeed in calling himself always to mind.
Action has consequence, and though his face
has faded into the country of the lost,
I look at my hand and see the injured place.

Like hasty marks on an explorer's chart:
this white stream bed, this blue lake on my knee
are an angry doctor at midnight, or a girl
looking at the blood and trying not to see
what we both have seen. Most of my body lives,
but the scars are dead like the grooving of a frown,
cannot be changed, and ceaselessly record
how much of me is already written down.

Part Song, With Concert of Recorders

1.

She   Doctor, I did not see that you were there.

He   Madam, I've stabbed your husband in his bed.
He now makes one with the unhouseled dead.
I come to have you tell me that you care.

She   You know I care.

2.

She   I did not know you when you came in there.

He   I did not then intend that you should know,
thought in the dark I'd have my way and go,
but love has come upon me and I care.

She   Tell me you care.

3.

She   Who made you come and find the door to there?
Who made you turn that handle and come in?
What we have done, what we do, it is sin;
we shall be punished for it; have a care.

He   I cannot care.

4.

She   And I, who lay so warm and quiet there—

He   And you, who grew excited with my kiss—

She   Who would have thought that it would come to this?
Let all be circumspect before they care.

He   But let them care.

5.

She   And he lies dead—

He   His blood is seeping there—

She   Where we have kissed—

He   Where we have done much more—

She   I liked it best the way it was before.

He   You like it now.

She   I like it, but I care.

He   No longer care.

6.

Both For we have gone a curious way from there,
but we have love and so we go ahead.
It does no good to think about the dead.
What's dead is dead, it can no longer care
as we can care.

7.

She Come, Doctor, we must fly someotherwhere.

He I have my bag full of essential things,
false passports, currency, and diamond rings—

She True pledge of love for those who truly care.

He Who love and care.

One Incident of Many

Turning clumsily into the embrace
she finds herself stopped by uncertainty.
It is not so dark that she cannot see his face
looking up into the rain. Can he suppose that she
came toward this kiss without encouragement?
Has she been reading into his every act
what she wants, and only cold kindliness was meant?

The night is like a tunnel around her head.
She is in love, it is the time for her
to be reassured. He is like something dead.
Surely if she speaks that nothingness will stir,
take her in its arms, be man, sweat and desire,
show her the mutual fire to her fire.

She is quiet. It was wrong to want what anyone gets.
No, he will say, somehow you've misunderstood.
If she beats her hands against him he will be good,
saying, it was my fault, saying, one forgets
how it is. She has forgotten herself again,
thinking something important had supplanted her.
She is as ignorant as ever, and as plain.

The night will pass, with its possibility;
the trees that seemed for a moment neutral there
in the fresh burst of the stayed, certain air
will lash and cringe around her face as she
turns up the path she has turned up before,
hurries, holding her coat about her head.
He need not trouble to see her to her door.

G.F. Died 1954, Aged 27

. . . e parve di costoro
quegli che vince e non colui che perde.

Now deeply drunk, always where you have found him
in any place before, he will lie dead,
thin hair spilt in a yellow pool around him
beneath the night light, his arms under his head,
his face jerks with the quickening dream that holds him.

He looked for people to kiss. Someone uncertain called him
to a hidden door less innocent than his eyes.
The lingering smile of that red-lit night appalled him,
but whirled him, after his nausea of surprise,
into the pattern of the dream that holds him.

Now he moves downward. Hundreds of mouths beside him
spit truths at his too-knowledgeable face;
hearing the hot birds and the voices of beasts deride him
he weaves helplessly, cries, stumbles out of this place
over the threshold, into the dream that holds him.

He dies in the body. The various bones that made him
loose gradually from their connected forms.
The shape of flesh that mimicked him and hid him
ruins past the touch of sensual alarms,
commends him, finally, into the dream that holds him.

Maybe all are angels there, and soar together
on steep wings, day after day speaking of love,
or in the hushed nights of deep, motionless weather
lie by each other gently kissing, and move
like white stars into the dark of the dream that holds them.

Things Kept

From the years
when cars were worth looking at,
when they sat the road with dignity and aplomb,
a hint of nautical danger in their construction,
now a parade of ten, a dozen
elegant dragons
moves down the street under its own deliberate power,
with wire wheels spinning, or immensely solid wheels
painted in sulphur yellow,
with collapsible roofs thrown back
like elbows akimbo, resting in thorough ease.

Even in the most empty day
creation can happen, and the ancient cars,
the Pyramids on wheels, the ruins of the Forum mobile,
a sudden fragment of Minoan Greek translated,
shine forth in the pure faith of restoration,
spin merrily forward, with the wholesome noise
of intimate, personal engines.
Red on red,
deep blue picked out with brass,
polished beyond fear of time or road stains,
they lavish in undecided weather
the beauty of making and keeping.

I can remember
sitting, reading a book, in early summer
on a stone terrace, at my right hand a weir,
and looking up to a ring of inquisitive peacocks,
six tame peacocks, trailing their tails in sequence,
tilting to one side their blue anachronous heads;

behind them, over the narrow, ruffled water,
on a small island, a stern stone lion, crowned,
remembering back toward the pulse of royal ages.
Their questions about me satisfied, the peacocks
took heavily to air, long trains depending,
and slowly flew through the pale sun to join him.

Objects, beings that have
the passion and flower of beauty caught about them,
the great design, rising, of peacock feathers,
the sculptured wheel of the maker's admiration,
the bold brass headlamp, the lion, defying night
and the dull years' ability to extinguish,
stand like right faith on their undoubted islands,
or move as gods move, powerful, of clear color,
meaning themselves and the virtue of their being,
bright coachwork tuned, wheels flashing, hackles raised
to hold strongly their inheritance of distinction,
blood relics of an ampler dispensation,
pure peacock blue, brass glory, furious stone.

The Self Prepares for an Unwilling Journey

The Dioscuri guard you in this passing;
being half of heaven and half of hell they know
what hurries you to your shamefaced undressing,
why your respectable fingers rattle so.

Though night, touched by a bulb that grimes the ceiling,
is in you and around you where you stand,
you cannot hope for any new concealing;
this hand that reaches for you is your hand,

this body yours that has been twin in anger
and that walked out of you and lived apart
doing violence to the accepted stranger;
leaving you peaceful in your arbored heart,

spinning and smiling as the world diminished,
as the great rages beckoned, but swept past.
The dog howls at the doorstop. This is finished.
Now you are in the room of the very last

and have the perfect partner for your dances,
knowing the steps that no one else has known,
the opened minutes and regretted chances,
knowing you to the engraving of your bone.

The Dioscuri guide you to your bedding.
Twice-fixed in heaven and hell, they see, and send
impossible starlight to describe your wedding,
and the long fire to reconcile your friend.

Silver Creek Falls

Watching the stream come spilling over its ledge,
the very point where it falls, your eyesight changes.
Only in idea is there such an edge,
a dividing line, because the water lunges
past it all of the time and is not the same.
Form is the slave of motion, not its king,
and what we name as if it had an object's name
is only an accident of that journeying.

Turn, having looked too long, and you cannot find
even shadows of the world you called your own;
interior shadows marry in your mind
with the swift circumstance of changing stone,
and your dimension is to recognize
elements in their own continual air:
outside the apparatus of your eyes
the water that only by vanishing is there.

The Lady of Shalott, Her Mirror Broken

Species of common garden cat, who are
you moaning for among the vegetables?
Your ears lie geometrically flat,

flat as the tops of innumerable strait tables;
and your mouth bursts with its interminable cry
in the growing voices that the garden babbles

of vine and weed and bean you break. And why?
There is no love lies hidden in its heart,
but the squat stone god Terminus stands smiling by,

telling you of ends and boundaries and part
of the ways you cannot get out and no one in.
Will you stop it now? There was no reason to start.

There's no outside, no others, nothing in
all of your life left empty; strut and stride
here in the carrots where you can keep clean

like the proper guardian of a proper pride.

The Læstrygonians

Our ship (in this easy metaphor I employ
calling life a voyage, calling experience cities)
came next to the country of the Læstrygonians.

They desired us as food. It was improper
so to be desired, but not unwelcome.
Men sometimes wish to become standing rib roasts.

And at least this desire could be gratified simply,
being a simple appetite. I mouthed an apple.
My colleagues coated themselves with mint sauce.

Whatever flesh the Læstrygonians
most nourished on, we were decided to be.
The intention was to rectify past error,

faults of the compass, distortions of parallax,
agreement to disagree, everything that had led
us increasingly toward a geography of abstraction.

We prepared the feast. The wise Læstrygonians,
understanding the virtue of their primitive fury,
withdrew to sea-caves, refused the invitation.

Uneaten, absorbed by nothing, we sailed on,
our ship an example of solipsism by day,
of the space in atomic nuclei, by night.

Stranger, sea-begrimed traveller from an unknown city,
advise us, you whose arms are only the oars' extension,
you who change plain bread into pure rowing daily,

into what language should we translate ourselves?
What form of thought will make us a form of flesh
right to be eaten by the Læstrygonians?

cursed for a male witch,
eyes superstitiously full,
flesh softer than human,
"having become himself
his fiction's hero" may
dance to a smart blaze,
staccato feet bound
fast to the fire's end,
his clumsy hands told
gestures of departure.

Why worry, lovey? He,
mother in her fat tomb,
auntie on her pension,
Kansas City an act done
in an indecent story,
now suffers his own air,
breathes himself wholly.
And if he takes off
all his clothes, smarts
in another country's love, if
he takes off his heart, bleeds
untranslated blood, still
it is his story.

But I agree, I
cannot leave it there, and
wait the improbable card
postmarked Champs Elysées:
"Everything dandy, death
easily managed. Find

fine company, Ambrose Bierce,
others who disappeared
dropping by for a drink.
Having become themselves
their fictions, are
spoken by new tongues.
Write to me. Love me. Yours."

Love among the Manichees

The blond cowl terse as a blunt threat to injure,
the claws instinctive to a triggering nerve,
I am a shut spring in my fanged disguises,
aping the beast I serve.

I would be for you an offering of clear spirit,
like water glistening over your spread hands,
like the pattern described in air when the bird has left it,
like not yet peopled lands.

Tick-laden fur ruffling for winds of danger,
I gorge on honey in the fallen tree,
snarl at approachers to these laden acres
that bind their fruit to me.

I would be for you like a length of fallow
from the earliest world, like open mountainside
too high for the spurred seed to beat and follow,
for the edged wing to glide.

Puzzled, the shared beast lurks under my eyelids,
mute, menacing, not able to let go,
or to conceive that who comes unconstrainèd
stays the most easily so.

I would be for you as a willing mirror,
plain crystal, undefined, of itself dumb,
that shapes its voice when you first look into it,
smiling, "Now you have come."

II

At Your
Old House

Chickens in San Francisco

*San Francisco. You can have four animals total. If you
have a dog and a cat, you could only have four chickens.*
—Sunset, *March 1974*

In aerobatics, white, red, speckled & spectacular
as if any spot on earth were the pin's bottom
of an enormous cage opening up to chicken heaven,
in a blur of parts, the eyes fringed and knowing,
the oviducts popping white eggs, brown, an eternal Easter,
hens running flat-footed, hysterical, the roosters up
in a little air, down, the scream, contentment,
chickens frying omelets, stuffing feather pillows, whirling
into feather fights, a believable feather winter . . .

If I kept chickens, that is how I would keep chickens.

Deduct the cat and the dog, which are imaginary,
and you have two chickens, a male chicken and a female chicken
(chicken sexing is high paid work, but you have to travel).
They are walking around the deck. They are Plymouth Rocks.
The male chicken wears a buckled hat and carries a shotgun
and the female chicken has the New England ABC:
A is for Abstinence, B is for Boils, C is for Colonel Sanders.
The chickens look terribly sparse on the windy deck
as if born plucked. They look at each other,
conscious of a hidden camera. They approach a cabbage
and under it they discover Shirley Temple.
They register the salvation of the race.
Shirley clucks a little, she is well into
what they call the skin of the part . . .

Oh cut, cut, cut, cut, cut. I feel about chickens
the opposite of the way San Francisco feels.
I feel about chickens, I feel about other animals
the way Colette felt about truffles. It is no good having any
unless you can have too much.

At Your Old House

1.

Fretful and sick, you ask
"Do they remember me
at my old house?"

Illness makes believable
all desertions; I
might die, love someone else.

If the world failed that way
it would help to think
you could go back

ignoring all those years
that tried to tell us we
lived in the same place.

2.

Yes, they remember you,
would have to, even though
the photographs are burned

of your hair done the old way
of your dark husband in
his young uniform.

Having loved you they
cannot will themselves
to entire indifference

but turn in the night sometimes
when your light step
touches their dream.

3.

"Do they remember me?
Would they believe me if
in my thin summer dress

I should go back to them
saying the years between
held no authority?

saying I knew myself
even from childhood, still
uninterrupted, still the same

and that I needed them
in that remembered world
still to stay the same?"

4.

No, the night has gone
where you left them; marks blur
of the fire

on the riverbank.
Rain and the winter's ice
wash them away.

And the figures have stood, turned,
begun to walk down the streets
of new towns

where you cannot be heard
now, with your far voice
calling their names.

5.

Fretful and sick, you long
for reassurance, want
everyone to forgive

what is not unforgivable,
only no longer there·
to be forgiven. Caught

in their own time
faces have changed,
lips spoken assurances

to a new night
in which the agreements of the body
have been re-made.

6.

Nevertheless, sleep.
And as your eyes close
in hurt uneasiness,

as your face grows
hot, like a child's
under the weight of the dream

I whisper to you that
even when their voices sound
unreachably far away

they still remember you,
your laughter, how you were
at your old house.

The History of the Moon

In people, nothing is clear. They knot together
and a steam comes up from them and hides them.

Their lettering is tribal, hard to read
unless you allow them the ownership of your closest blood.

More and more each year the refracted moonlight
slivers among them: which shadows are its sure shadows?

Goodbye children. If we meet from now on it will be
in the light of the crystal lattice of an equation.

History begins where I leave you. The historical moon
is a mountain of stone piled upon stone piled upon stone.

The Anniversary

It was your smell that, for a day after, I carried with me.
My body smelled not of me but of you. The train
ticked over its crossings, stopped. In all its noises
I heard, suddenly and bewilderingly, your voice.

That was six years ago, the damp riverbank,
the Midwest storms massed, raining like an indictment,
the attacks of telephones, old interruptions talking.
Out of that, at your voice, I came to this different world.

Now, with the formal furniture, the black puppy quietly
lying at the door, the flames of the candles steady,
we are held by our reflections in the rose-colored wine—
a civilization of agreements, a closed place.

Thousands of miles away, the summer storms
still race in their green light. The night trains hurry on
across Canada, their noise empty of voices.
The old telephones busy themselves with the old words.

Here, in the Pacific evening, the puppy stands up
suddenly in the doorway and barks toward the dark street,
protecting what has come to include him. Six years now.
I cannot tell his voice from the room's voice.

I cannot tell your voice from my own voice.

For Every Last Batch
When the Next One Comes Along

Next door they've finally brought home the new baby.
Well, my wife says, carrying him over carefully
for a tour of inspection, would you look at that for two weeks!

It's true he's a good baby, big, fine head of hair.
Look, says my wife, his navel's healed up already
and his you-know-what's bigger than the two-year-old's.

I don't hear much from this baby late at night.
He's too big to be fretful; fill him up with milk
and he just hums comfortably on through till morning

while his two-year-old brother cries, deliberately
wets, goes babyish, tries to crawl into bed with
mother and daddy, get back into their flesh,

all of which is anathema to the pediatrician
who knows how the two-year-old statistically
can't be allowed to slide. Up, two-year-old!

Let's get you back on your feet while there's still time.
The world's no raisin bun aimed straight at you.
There's always another contender for the playpen.

Though I still feel sympathy for you. Who ever wanted
that excessive baby? Who wanted him to arrive
with that vulgar head of hair? Who wanted him to be

carried around the neighborhood, the mothers saying:
Big babies are good babies; would you look at that perfect navel!
Would you ever believe the size of his you-know-what!

Virginia Woolf Gathers Mushrooms

She is not easy to see. She wears
something anonymous: not the dress
she has not got and so (sigh of relief)
cannot go to the party she was
so much of two minds about going to.
Certainly not the dress she wore down
to dinner at Hyde Park Gate, after
washing in the inadequate basin, the dress
her half-brother, that authority,
looked at and looked away.

The mushrooms are not
really an obsession, but, as the war
keeps killing and removing, as the moon
becomes a mere indicator (if it is bright
there will be German planes, the servants
on mattresses in the basement) there is
little enough to hope for, little
that seems convincing
in any natural way.

Chocolate is unobtainable, eggs arrive
by two, if they arrive. But on the slope
above Asheham, at the right time of the year,
the mushrooms are given. There are the right places
to find them, learned only by craft and care.
Some visitors (Pernel Strachey, Vice-President
of Newnham College, Cambridge) look too high.
The trick is to focus in.

The years gone, it is easy to imagine her,
that historic profile, attending to the best music,
dividing and discriminating, allowed for once
the right dress, the right hat, the clothes
one discriminates in.

            Harder
to watch her carry her almost-nothing body
up the earth slope, taking on an earthen color,
vanishing almost from the over-freighted air,
to watch where yesterday
there was nothing; today, something.
In a little dip of the hill, enough mushrooms

to fill her handkerchief, enough
for two people to eat, quietly, at evening,
love continuing, life happening,
the house easy so.

More under Saturn

Of course it sounds cold.
It is cold.
Every year spent on the ground draws that much more of the first warmth
    from our bodies.

What did you think would insulate you against time?

    • • •

I walk out into the winter garden.
It is the root vegetables—
beets, potatoes—
the russet apples wrapped separately in newspapers and packed in old barrels
on which we live.

    • • •

              Dead cabbage stalks
that grew up fast out of the fleshy, leafy fruit
stand like a field of dry clubs.

Who's there, to hit at?

    • • •

The sky appears to be indifferent. If it spoke,
"Love me," it would say, "You keep alive from now on
only on how much of me you can refuse to hate."

Therefore

Nothing exists that is not marred; therefore
we are obliged to imagine how things might be:
the sea
at its green uttermost, the shore
white to exaggeration, white before
it was checked and clouded by its spent debris.

Nothing exists that does not end, and so
to knowledge we must deliberately be untrue:
you
murmuring that you will not go, when you will go,
promising to do always what you cannot do:
hold the sun steady, and the sky new.

No one exists who can be loved the same
by day as by dark; it is that sleeping place,
lame,
we attempt to follow into, and cannot trace,
that makes us lie, saying we know his face,
as if we knew even half of his true name.

In the Dreaming

*Indeed, there seems to have been a continual preoccupation
with the mystery of life and death, and all that was unknown
or not present was referred to as being "in the dreaming."*
　　　　　　　　—Alan Moorhead, The Fatal Impact

1.

In the dreaming
we walk through the streets of Oxford
hand in hand.
I am able to let you touch me,
to be glad.

Voices laugh around us
in the dark almost dawn
hurrying toward the river
and the May morning.

Perhaps even the ghost
of our unborn child,
male, stirs,
smiles in his twelve-year sleep.

2.

Here, in the summer city,
I lie in bed, closing
darkness about my mind,

closing doors, windows,
hiding
where hiding's possible,

not able to taste
in the sky
the weather turning.

3.

At Maganosc
in the stone bedroom
waked
by some dream of loss

the terraces of vines
steep outside
in the green dark

you came naked to me
through midnight,
frightened and confident

safe in our same bed.

4.

We meet, eating, smoking,
talking of therapists or friends,
looking through thick glass windows
at the impractical sea.

The seeds of death always between us
on the plastic table.

I try to will myself
not to pick them up.

What do I remember?
You asked once to be
buried beside your mother.

5.

If forgiveness comes
it will be gradual.

Subtle
and loose as smoke.

A little lessening
of this grim year.

6.

Thinking of me,

think of what was

and of what in it
there might have been.

Nothing is thrown away.
Nothing is lost, not
the most awkward kiss,
not
viciousness, rage.

All are still there,
loving you as they can,
wise, in the heart's night,

all there, in the dreaming.

Androids

Androids
are not different in appearance
from you and me
except they are more beautiful.
Male-type androids are muscular,
have smooth chests,
and incredible apparatus;
the female-type
are, as we say, pneumatic,
and have been taught everything about it
there is to know.

You have been to bed
with an android, probably thinking
"Jesus, did I luck out!" The android
is not really thinking about you at all.
It is gathering information
for the data bank.

As you fall back,
exhausted, unsuspicious,
the android will kiss your forehead.
It will murmur "Thank you."
And then it will leave.
It is a characteristic of androids
not to stay on till morning.

And even if you *were* suspicious
it would do you little good.
The only way to identify the android

is to look inside its navel
where it is stamped
with its country of manufacture.

That is why it leaves while you are exhausted.
It is important to it
not to let you get that close.

Die Älte Frau, Die Älte Marschallin

Of the three voices, it is hers that stays.

The lovers leave the stage. They have become
a shape of their own, perhaps not a lasting one
but enough for now.

                        Who does not know their world,
the thrones, the feasts,
the wealth and accomplishments that warm like day?
Who has not slept in that bed, made out of the breasts
of nightingales? Who has not touched
delicacy so ideal it is feather, neither bone?

But they have left. The stage now is hers alone.

She has been them, to come here. She has sung
innocent Sophie, Octavian the youthful lover.
Girl to young man to someone who is outside sex.
Die älte Frau, die älte Marschallin.
The old woman, the old woman who is in love.

But then with what, we ask, because she is alone
on the stage. Is it that she loves herself?
Is it, God forbid, her impertinent Negro page?
Is it age? We might understand that affair,
love gestures stroking unresponsive air,
smiles that make smiling into an offense,
that loss of sense to sense.

No, dear, it is the music, the generosity.
She is in the music alone, it is her place.
She has come to it out of the romances:
girl, boy, the carrier of the silver rose,
the prince of chances.
Now she folds into herself. It is her repose.
She advances.

Having had the stage to herself, she lets it go.
For a moment everything is empty. Her page,
quick as an eyelash, comes on to recover
her handkerchief.

                         Somewhere, a lover
turns in the night, knowing that he will age.

We know, we know, love. Here is the empty stage.

Alligators and Paris and North America

For Adrianne on her birthday

*Bernice Dewey going to the Snyder trial, then coming back and
hypnotizing her alligator, which she kept in the tub and which Dos
Passos said was rather limp from having been hypnotized so much.*

No, darling, the world is not ruled by sense, not sense.
For every statue of George Washington making laws
in every city, there is in some back room
Bernice Dewey hypnotizing her alligator,
she intent and glittering, the uneasy reptile
hoping it is all a dream, that it will wake
back in the Everglades.

            I walked down Stockton
Street toward Market. It was a reasonable day.
But when I looked to my right, there walking beside me
was a six-foot carrot, quite casual, taking the air.
I looked helplessly to my left, to a six-foot mushroom.
It was no time for composure. I almost ran.
Nobody had told me about the new health-food store
that was opening that day. Turning onto Stockton,
coming up to meet me in the most deliberate way
were two men sitting inside a large football helmet.
I caught a bus and went home. It was not my day.

Darling, not sense. I don't know why it is.
But why, when the plastic zipper of my trousers broke
in the I. Magnin dressing room, and the disdainful attendant

gave me four brass safety-pins to put myself back together,
and you asked him what was taking so long, why did he say
"I'm afraid, Madam, that he has had an accident." That day
I went back to the parking garage and backed the car
straight into a pillar. An attendant on a moped
looked at me curiously and looked away.

> *Having acquired the necessary training, Mary Cassatt was hung
> in the prestigious Paris Salon for five consecutive years, no mean
> distinction for any painter, let alone an American woman.*

I know he is right. If he had meant hanged
he would have said hanged, yet I cannot help seeing her
with resistless decorum through those five long years,
her skirts neat and even her feet held
effortlessly in the first position of ballet,
hanging on the museum wall. What would be
"the necessary training" and how would one acquire it?
Perhaps in a Paris studio, day by day
inching a little farther up the wall,
doing Yoga to help it all, pulling away
mentally and physically from the unnecessary floor.
If our lives are supposed to be art, that would be one way:
to become the picture. It would be "no mean distinction."
You are an American woman. What would you say?

My earliest episode of conscious frigidity—that is, of frigidity
after the fact of accepting my homosexuality and after spells of
being quite comfortable with it—occurred in a bathtub on 17th
and Market streets in San Francisco . . .

There it is, the bathtub motif recurs.
The limp alligator, the limp homosexual. Are we all hypnotized?
What is that bathtub doing in the street—
a busy intersection, as it happens,
where all of the streetcars turn?

Conscious frigidity. It sounds like something
achieved, rather than come across by chance.
This is my friend, Conscious Frigidity.
He/she is an avatar of Shiva the Destroyer.
I am happy to meet you, Avatar. I hope you can drink vodka.
There is an alligator in the bathroom named Bernice Dewey.
I mean the bathroom is named Bernice Dewey.
For some reason, the alligator keeps trying to escape.
Even to hypnotism, it keeps saying, there must be an end.
Friend, if you are friend, take me away.
Let us sail this bathtub straight out of 17th and Market
into the awakening day.

When he went on to sing "I send thee a gift of roses," however, and
attempted to cast some artificial flowers into the audience, the wire
stems got caught in his bodice, so that he had to keep pulling at
them—like something in a dream, Bodfish said, when all your
powers become paralyzed and you can't accomplish anything.

Roses were the wrong choice. No wonder the wires got caught
"like something in a dream." I dreamed of reason
in the way that Goya did, and found the same
ruin, the same pitilessness, the same shame.
It is not sense, darling, that regulates us.
If I offer you flowers, are they flowers that can speak their name?
Or does it matter, as long as they are not tame?
Now it is spring, the camellias are in bloom.
On the sheltered deck, the Japanese maple
puts out new leaves as if it had perfect faith.
How does a flower feel when it tries to break
from its still internal shape?
How does a leaf feel its shape, as the closed fan stretches?
Like a man stretching his arms up into the air,
yawning, yawning so loud it is pure vigor,
brings the hair to attention, prick
to alertness, eyes sidling around the bar the old way.
Darling, not sense, but something that has its say.

The wire stems caught in his bodice. I could cry.
He is trying so, and so failing as he tries.
I see him with his eyes
averted, and with a sick flush rising.
He has done it wrong. There was the advertising

and now he has messed it up. It was not his day.
It is nonsense. It was nonsense from the start.
Defeated, determined, dead.
And still, for all of its awkwardness, sincere.
A fool being a fool in his own way.

*Margaret's uncle had invested in $10,000 worth of fireworks and
set them off in the Bois de Boulogne, and then killed himself.
(Dorothy Parker said, when I told her about this: "And those bum
French fireworks—probably only a fourth of them went off!") An
aunt used to sit at her window and drop ink on people in the street.*

It is not sense. Why do I keep expecting that?
The mad old aunt
drops ink (Ink?) on the people in the street.
Where does she get the ink? A trust fund, maybe.
It is the same wild kind of determination.
Bernice Dewey hypnotizing her alligator, the old aunt
deliberately, close in on target, dropping ink.
I imagine she would have chosen dove-grey hats,
or the shoulders of very expensive prostitutes,
who would look at their carefully powdered shoulders, think
"I have done wrong." Or that is what she would think.
Sleeps well at night, like anyone with a plan.

Tonight, ten thousand dollars' worth
of fireworks will destroy the Bois de Boulogne.
Clutching the last rocket, there will be a mad old man
trying to get to Heaven if he can.

He will have spent
the whole damn heritage, down to the last *pourboire.*

All to have fire. It is not sense at all.
But the fire-fall
climbs to its ultimate, destroys, descends.
It has its own bright ends.
So near, so far.
All that we are, and what we think we are.

(Quotations in the poem are from Edmund Wilson, *The Twenties,* ed. Leon Edel;
John Barkham, a review in the *San Francisco Chronicle;* G. J. Hoisington, an article
in *Gay Sunshine.*)

The Rainbow Grocery

You don't find it for yourself. Someone takes you.
The bars have shut down and still it is not time.
Whatever was going to happen is lost in the smoke
and the old booze, of the people who made it leaving together.
Of the quiet that comes when you've said it. Nothing to say.
That's the time of night for The Rainbow Grocery.

And it looks like nothing, like nowhere on God's earth,
like an old place abandoned. It is abandoned
but the abandoned door opens, onto a lobby
of wax derelicts, grey as the uncertain night.
No one human has sat in these chairs. No one human.
The lights are yellow and they are ready to die.

You pay a dollar to get in. Then
there's a place to check your valuables. Then
there is a dusty hall which might lead: where?
Then down a staircase to a grimy basement.
You can get coffee or soft drinks if you really want them.
That's the room where men are dancing only with men.

Past that is what it's all about: the black room.
You walk past its door and you know it's full of people,
people you can't see and were never meant to see,
hands touching you, chests, bellies, the shy night.
And if you are stripped, sucked, and the rest done to you,
The Rainbow Grocery will have taken you in.

Always at the end of a hall, of a dark hall
where there is a next room, always a next room,

and who knows what's sleeping there, then or forever?
Always when the bars close, somebody says:
"Why don't we go down to The Rainbow Grocery?
You haven't been there? I can get you in."

The Heroine

Here we heard that captains of schooners which had arrived
from Hawaii, report that a light is visible on the terminal crater
of Mauna Loa, 14,000 feet above the sea, that Kilauea, the flank
crater, is unusually active, and that several severe shocks of
earthquake have been felt. This is exciting news.
       —*Isabella L. Bird,* Six Months in the Sandwich Islands

She arrives at the volcano almost dead,
the enormous modesty of her skirts, torn, drenched, dragging her back,
and the sickness, whatever it is she travels to get away from, preventing her.
The rocks, the rain, the night relapse into violence,
into the self-centered brutality of an adolescent world.
She has to go there.

Her family is good. She is of independent means.
The missionaries respect her.
And she does believe. Those are in fact real psalms
in which she participates, a real God living in loving-kindness
justice made merciful, with a truly Christian people.
In the midst of that, the mouth of the night demands her

and she must go, with an unsympathetic woman, not English,
and a guide partly reluctant, part threatening,
part not determinable, into the chaotic lava,
flows, tubes, a landscape of black intestines
that has hardened only the moment she looked at it.
She must go beyond that
to where it is all change.

Later on, to the mild surprise of her friends, she will contract
a suitable marriage. Her husband will be
something of an invalid, but not tedious about it.
Inheld by the intricate whalebone of her convention
she will, the heroine, accepting concede herself
into age, into a world it is hard to say
she had abandoned . . .

                              who still
in that western ocean that went on forever
had not been able not to go to encounter
an entire whale hanging for a miraculous second
in necessary, unsupportive air, before it crashed back
like an explosion into what we think of
as its natural element . . .

                              who still
in that other necessary part of her mind and place
had moved restlessly, encumbered, across those thousands of miles
to sit in a raw town almost outside the world,
waiting for news from the interior
or what, for her life, she was obliged to see:

the rightness of an extreme, the island burning.

His Death from Cancer

I dig my foot into the stubborn grass.
I look to where the stellar jays, by two,
figure in anger about their threatened nest.
He, a high shape of water, walks
across his attentive lawn and disappears.

Let us make, in fear, a disarray
of the sheets, let us make love until
it is hard to tell which breath comes from which body.
Nipple to nipple, let us exhaust the clock
until no time is available for his going.

I will make him, as with no preliminaries
I explore you, live. I will make him
a language it is not possible not to talk in.
I will bring him to the bewilderment of being.
I will be fed by him, I will be fed.

The grass abstains. It knows when it is evening.
And you lie back, your muscles lessening towards
anatomy. All the birds of the beleaguered air
hum into their light-belled bones and hang asleep.
It is the accountant's hour.

The construction of memory begins. Now there, now here,
I half-realize his absence, as we lie
counting the generations, recognizing
how alone it is to be the oldest living,
unprotected against the hard newness of the sky.

A Kindness

Where did we stop? In dead summer, that is
male, yellow. You stripped into that glare
of live gold.
It was like living in gold to try to touch you.
It was as if you were day.

Nothing of this is true, but will you
let me have it, Imaginary?

The laugh, confidence, the symmetrical clean
body capable of itself, so being body
as to be naked even to the hands. Will you give me that?

Because even if it is not true, I need
something now to look back to, in order to say:
I have been sudden in the sun's perfection,
I have had blood rise like light,
my hands have answered,
my memory is a bush of grown flame.

It is a kindness you can do me, to have been there
at the center of summer, yourself the attack of summer,
and to have made all that light out of being young.

I need to have loved you. I need to have told you so.

Face-Paintings of the Caduveo Indians

The face-paintings of the Caduveo, says Levi-Strauss,
reflect a society they have forgotten:
like heraldry, he says, like playing cards.

It is like that. Even my mother, now,
turning the pages of the photograph album,
forgets the older faces. She insists she remembers,
but what she remembers is a style of face,
a way she can remember people looking.

I saw you at the Greek Orthodox Church on Sunday.
You had lost weight. I was drinking sweetened coffee.
We were no longer a society.
I saw you as a stranger might, with interest.
You had drawn back behind the surface of your face.

In the last days, having nothing in common, we played cards,
and the cards became their own society,
playing themselves, not responsible to the players.
Your face was new, as if it had not been used.

I do not know what became of the Caduveo.
The face-paintings are in a museum, with the relics
of other societies that forgot themselves,
that became too few to be able to remember.

It is like that: a lessening of chances,
the thought that I will never again be in love
but will sit foolishly waiting for what is in the cards
while your face becomes a photograph, becomes
only a way I remember people looking.

III

Gambling
at Reno

Gambling at Reno

Playing the quarter slots
my hands take on
the color of money:
something between grey and silver.
A cast over the skin.

This time I am not drinking,
though the drinks are offered.

I do not expect to win.

Still, moving
to the dollar machine
that is taller than I am
and has a handle
like an arm you encounter in love,
that you pull and it responds
and comes back to you,

I am asking it, yes, this one time.
And for a while
it fills all the pockets of my safari jacket
with dollars.

And I begin to think, it likes me.
This thing with five rows of flashing lights
wants me. It becomes personal.
Am I not taking its hand in mine?
Are we not, as I hope, I hope,
moving together?

A little audience has gathered.
I am winning, they want to know
why? What have the machine and I
found in one another? These are the *voyeurs,*
the unsuccessful. The bad lovers.
I am the good lover.

For a while the machine thinks so.
Then, as with all these affairs,
it retrieves what it has contributed.

It refuses me.

Seven women in flowered hats
take over. The machine is indifferent now.
They take its hand mechanically, chewing gum.
How can it pretend it recognizes them?

I am angry with it. It was my machine.
It is not angry but tired. It has had a whole day
standing on its feet and rejecting lovers.

Performances

In a fright-wig
that is his own hair,
the public poet
drinks from a bottle
labelled ostentatiously: GIN.
He introduces
his sexual collie, Mary.
They hump together.
His audience
claps rhythmically.

The rock singer
so into himself
as to have come out
the other side,
unzips, masturbates
on stage, masturbates
in a coffee shop, on tour,
using pancake syrup
for lubricant.
Boys or girls scream.

A crowd gathers.
The wild, simpering
twenty-year-old
dances on the parapet
naked, fakes
swan dives
to the sweet concrete.
The street
fills up with flashers.

Their trench coats
lit suddenly
as if by lightning
they give their gods away.

In the back seat
of the patrol car
the drunk driver
who has killed
two elderly women
looks up
at the white egg-faces
crowding the windows,
smiles tentatively,
begins a gesture
of propitiation
that has no middle
nor end.

The lion eats
its insufferable tamer
and the crowd roars.
Then the crowd eats
the lion, belches,
rumbles contentedly,
goes home in twos
more than ready
to strip each other,
tangle into sex.
Strings up their blood.

Behind stage,
gutted, the performers
wipe blood from
their feet, mouths,
congratulate each other
on how well it went,
how the whole fabric
of the tent
shuddered with applause.

They will do it
again, pecking
at the lever
that releases them.
They will gather
again, after
the performance,
examining with
professional detachment
who did not die enough,
who can give
more than he gave,
who has a little
place in him
not yet explored
into which
the perfect audience
still has room to go.

Confidence

1.

Dark and intent, you sit
on the bar stool beside me,
your sharp Italian face
beautiful with persuasion.

The cat's arch of your back
curves forward to what you want:
you can get 200 bucks tonight
if I will stake you,

and it's so safe, only an hour,
a trip across town, a man who
is ready to buy. The final
assurance: "You could come with me."

That done, we could relax,
spend the whole weekend in bed
(you say you're good in bed)
not hustling, drinking.

How magnificently you go
out of yourself, you in your fine tie
and your white teeth, your expert eyes
in the poker pens of South City

all of you committed to what
you have to have, cursing
when it doesn't come, believing
it has to come

if you can convince me, your hand
casually on my arm, your voice
full of secrets.
How could they not be true?

I do what I knew I would, give in,
write you the check. You are all
thanks, confidence. Now for the errand.
Now you are on your way

2.

And as I knew it would, the first
telephone call comes back to the bar.
An hour later, the second.
Days later, the canceled check returns.

Dear Lee, I have lost
nothing I could not afford.
I have paid to be taken into
your risk, your complicity.

How wise you were, knowing
the precise dream that would move me:
to be lithe, young, lightly criminal,
to be hurrying through the night.

For a week it was like having
a dangerous brother, who loved me,
who could talk only to me, who
must whisper what he had to say, and go.

3.

Dark and intent, you sit
at the bar, now, in another city,
waiting for a man who will know you
almost before you speak,

who will watch with
love and amusement, as you display before him
the shuttle of your deft hands, as you find
the wish that unlocks him.

He will hear you say
in confidence: we both know
the bars we can score in.
He will hear you say

we can win, over
the fat woman in the eyeshade.
We can win
if we play the right cards.

Believing and disbelieving, he will give
you the check. He will have won
something he needed to have
even as you turn to go.

Afternoon Evening and Night in the Courtyard of the Museum of Modern Art

This monumental sculpture a
compound of many parts has been
assembled to destroy itself.

Cocktails and *hors d'oeuvres* are
available for the large number
of invited witnesses.

The sculpture begins des-
troying itself; hard to suppose
that it feels nothing

as it removes buttons, dials,
undertakes with one limb to
dissociate another limb.

The guests eye one
another speculatively, what
would happen if

everyone here in
black tie, pearls, submitted
to the same process?

It takes the sculpture eight
hard-working hours
to become rubble.

Over the elegant court-
yard of the museum where
this event is taking place

long stripped of atmosphere, pocked
by its history of accident
the moon rises.

"Look," say as many guests
as have lasted to the very end,
"at the moon smiling."

Life Moving More Rapidly
Than Hands Can Manage

That summer when I worked in the frozen foods plant
all the skin peeled off the soles of my feet.
I stood, in a slide of water, at the bottom
of an iron ramp, down which raspberry crates
came washing. With a foot-lever
I turned each one of them over, stacked them on pallets.

I dream still, sometimes, of being sent
with a scoop shovel into the zero room
where the twelve-inch pipe that carried frozen peas
had broken, and a steady cascade of peas
covered the floor, and kept rising around me
a little faster than I could shovel. Only a little.

It is in these littles that we are undone.
We are less fast than we should be, less knowledgeable.
The summer I was a window-dresser for Montgomery Ward
I knew nothing about plackets in women's skirts.
The mannequins got dressed, if they got dressed, by force.

True panic is a little concentric place
in which I know I have something to do, and know
there is no way I am going to do it in time.
Suicides are not triggered by vast love affairs,
but by the noise of the toilet, steadily leaking,
by the knowledge that you do not know how to make it stop.

Learn to cheat. It is easier
to ask questions on an examination than to answer them.
It is easier to hire a CPA
than to go yourself into the constricting chambers

of Internal Revenue, and shovel always
the wrong documents, not enough documents,
while the cold numbers rise about your calves and thighs.

Learn to be careful in love, choosing
a slow lover, someone whose micro-seconds
are longer than your own, and happen later.
Choose secretaries who misfile, keep them away
from familiarity with sophisticated machines.

Nevertheless, always, the frames will move
one frame faster than you can visualize.
On your back, in the experimental cubicle
where problems in mathematics are projected on the ceiling,
when you cannot solve the first problem, when time
is ticking loudly by you, your mouth sweet
with saliva gathering, lie.

The machines will know you lied. They will say to one another
on their instantaneous tapes: "He lied."
If they are feeling generous, they will only note
that fact. Then they will let you advance to the next problem.

Fred and the Holy Grail

He is busy destroying the landscape with lightning bolts,
so they ask him "What is your name, O Prophet?" He says, "Fred."
"O Fred," they respond, "will you help us find the Holy Grail?"

It seems right. By London time
it is four in the morning. This is the only bar
in the airport at Bangor, Maine.
The stall that sells lobsters is shut, all the shops are shut.
There is only the late show on TV, or to walk
among the strewn, dishevelled passengers who have passed customs.
Who knows how many are looking for the Holy Grail?
You need to be virgin. Who knows how many are virgin?
Even as their children collapse upon them, numbed with sleep.

Who knows what kind of customs they may have passed:
as, gone through and beyond, or, in another sense,
given to others. Fred is not so bizarre an inspector,
asking "What have you brought back? What are you going on with?"
The wrong answer, and there you are, destroyed.

St. Ursula went to Cologne with eleven thousand virgins,
all of whom were martyred there. Or else it is a misprint
in a mediaeval text, and there were only eleven virgins.
Nevertheless they were destroyed, though they may have had
in the moment of immolation, upheld before them
an image of white hands elevating the Holy Grail.

We do need help, even though Fred seems to be
an uncertain conductor, given to sudden rages.
If he came walking dangerously out

of the 25-inch screen, asking me to define,
perhaps to justify my customs, would I pass?

Six hours from now it will be Oakland airport
in the bitter morning air. I check again
to make sure I have my passport, American money,
the remains of the traveller's checks. Of course I have.

The movie is ending. Fred did agree to help,
though I thought he had reservations,
and every so often blasted something. A nervous tic?
Psychologically explainable? Capable of responding to treatment?

We climb, virgin or experienced,
back up into the plane, up into the air,
waiting for the stewardess to serve an unspeakable breakfast.
The moment has passed, this night, for the Holy Grail.

Here There Are Three of Us
Driving South in This Expensive Car

of whom two will make love. What happens
to the other? Is it for a reason of his own
that he is in this square, cage, situation?
Is it because he is the driver that he has lost tonight?
His little foot pumping at the little pedals,
his mouth opening toward what he thought
would have been words?

Being in love, even if it is not
being in love for long, is to establish
an exclusive bed, a place that can be defined only
by cruelty to another. Outside the englobed room,
the delicacies we must have to become lovers,
there is another figure, naked and unfortunate,
who wanted to be loved, and who did not succeed.

To be in love is almost too large a room
to be tolerable in, and we do not behave well.

To be unloved has at least the bruise of fact.
Say aloud, "I am unloved," and the night applauds.

The night must have someone left for itself, someone
apart from the dense, the satiated lovers.

It must have someone listening to whom
it can tell its long difficulties, its long aloneness.
Someone unsatisfied, to whom it believes it belongs.

You Cunning White Devils!

What is important about Tarzan is muscles, he is
a whole anatomy lesson right out there in the open
for every girl to see.

The task of the missionaries
as they saw it, was to get every bit of flesh
enveloped in clothing. God is not in his Heaven
until the Queen of Hawaii succumbs under crinolines.

The flower fainting into the intoxication of its own sweetness.
Mangoes making themselves sexually ready for the ripe mouth.
The Society for the Propagation of the Bible
translating, translating.

Me Tarzan, you Jane, you wanna make it?
And then that bird there, he come out of the shrubbery,
he say, me no bird anymore, you talk about me
anytime from now on, you call me The Holy Ghost.

Stella Dallas

Here he laid his finger upon the half-hour, and decided that
when the minute-hand reached that point he would go . . .
                    —*Virginia Woolf,* Night and Day

Stella stands in the rain, outside the great house,
lit with a thousand candles, in which her daughter,
whose name I have forgotten, is about to make
that triumphant marriage: duke, millionaire?
Stella holds the iron fence posts, topped with barbs.
She strains to see, until a bored policeman
asks her what she is doing there. "I only wanted,"
she says, "to see the pretty lady."
She is dismissed.

Stella remembers the careful birthday party,
the invitations that were sent out well on time,
the food, the favors,
the hours the two of them spent in that dining room
she had tried to make polite. The occasion
to which for some reason, some reason, no one came.

When you give a party, ask someone to come ahead
to wait with you. In the last half-hour,
when the turkey is carved and decorated, when the eggs
shimmer in their aspic, the old silver,
such as you have, is polished and made ready,
when you have collected whatever you have to offer,
will they come? Why is it so much in doubt?

Because, at the train station, standing under the clock,
watching people meet people they had intended to meet,
the time leans out toward you. You check your watch
furtively, knowing that everyone
in the whole world, watching you check your watch,
knows you will not be met, that there is no one there.

Later, in the bar, the smiling bartender
pretends not to notice as you check your watch.
When the minute hand reaches that point, you will go.
Then, when it reaches the next point, you will go.
The bartender, smiling, offers you a drink
on the house. You have been there that long.

So no one came. There is work, there is retribution.
Eventually you will be beautiful, well known,
with incredibly blonde hair. They will be sorry then.
The officious policeman will consider your identity
and recognize you immediately. He will say:
"What can I do for you, madame?" as the rain
falls steadily over what is present and is past.
He cannot come to your party, which is over.
Taking the white silk cloak about your shoulders
which are bare, dusted with sequins, you will say:
"You may call me a cab, officer. I came
only for a moment to look at the pretty lady."

Avalanche

1.

I have spent the whole day, or is it twenty years,
building up with you this conclusion, that totters
over our heads.

Let it slip, swing, the nominal body
purse itself for a second, and then discharge.
Ruin. How we have waited for it.

The chute, the white wave of massiveness
when nothing can be understood
or outvoted.

Millennia later, we will be chopped
out of a glacier. You will be wearing
a sign saying "You." I will be wearing,
frozen, allowable, an admiration.

We will each be classified according to our kinds.

2.

Here we are at however many feet
on the mountain: the South Face
which nobody has ever climbed.

It is night: we are crammed
side by side into linked sleeping capsules.
Everything is to survive.

That I have been in love with you
since the first time we met
will not surprise you.

Nor that you have been in love with another,
my rival, the chance-acceptor,
the isolate, playing his own game.

How do we survive? At morning
up toward the summit, there is a flurry of snow
and in it a shape, iceless, condescending.

It has been there before. It will win.

3.

The euphoria of sleep, as the cold
comes into and upon us.

Great shadows
walk from the white walls.
They are carrying white bells, white
mitres, white
everything that has to do with religion.
The whole mountain is fulfilled with nuns.

And I turn to you, asking
give me your blood, I need it.
Give me out of whatever entrenched,
solidified, shifting place we have got into,
give me your blood.

If it is a dream it is, as dreams are,
ambiguous. If it is a place
it is slipping into another place.
In the midst of the ice caverns, the ice crevasses,
the blue tunnels, the extraordinary,
let us hold together, if it can be done.

Ezekiel's Rabbit

The Lord God, bigger than the whole world,
hates us. Upon Jerusalem,
which has been disobedient, he will bring
the available plagues, all of the plagues there are.
And he will speak through the mouth of a man
he otherwise forces to be mute, a convenience.
Someone who is without choice an obedient vessel.

"Woe, woe, woe unto Jerusalem," says the Lord God.
He says it over and over, until I begin to feel
he has been too much indulged, an enormous infant
spitting at the teat that has so generously fed him.
He is old enough to play games, just old enough,
and so he picks up Ezekiel like a toy
and breaks him, and continues to break him.
Ezekiel recognizes he has been chosen as a prophet.

Into this scenario, let me introduce a rabbit.
I am sorry for Ezekiel, I would provide him a companion.
If it were a human companion, the Lord God
would dissolve it; it might speak, Ezekiel might speak.
The whole tantrum would have been wasted.
Jerusalem would go on with its normal business.

Even if I introduced one of the higher primates,
like an orangutan, the Lord God would be suspicious.
"What is this," he says, beating with his rattle
at the sides of the world, "that looks almost like a man
and might become a man? What is this that might speak?"
That is why Ezekiel is kept mute.
It is of speech that the Lord God is most jealous.

But a rabbit, until its cry of death,
is speechless. It is comfortable, it nibbles.
If Ezekiel is broken, it can come close to him.
It can lick his wounds.

And as Ezekiel travels, as he must travel,
goaded by the Lord God, stopped and started
like a mechanical train, opened and closed
as the Lord God decides to speak through him,
reduced to the stuttering diaphragm
of an early crystal set, labelled "Ezekiel,"
let him have attending on him a small animal,
to which, traitorously, he may feed carrots,
which he may take into his bed at night,
the poor, cold bed that a prophet must inhabit.

Let him have something of his own, mutilated and driven
by a force that says he is nothing of his own.
Let him touch something that is not Jerusalem.

Way up in the high sky the Lord God
knows when every sparrow falls; in fact, he kills them.
It is no more than an amusement.
What indeed can he have besides amusements?
He can never die, he cannot even grow old.
Today has no meaning to him, nor tomorrow.
On the same day he continually destroys Jerusalem.

How to subvert him except by giving our wills
to his measureless vanity, giving the keys and rings

from the secret pocket, giving him even the words
we had hoped to make love with, grow old in the company of.

Then, when he is bloated with the sleep of receiving,
forget for a moment Jerusalem, think,
in the still space left inside the words when even the words
have been given up, how if Ezekiel
intends love, something will offer itself to him
that he can love, something small, even his rabbit.

Dog under False Pretences

Not very affectionate; she likes to kiss,
but not to stay still long and be petted.
Yet if she is shut outside, she barks angrily.
If I move from one room to another, she moves too.
Is it a confusion in her history?

Now, after these months, I have her papers
from her first owner. Why was she given up?
The pet groomer who had her, and the birds, and Norman
the Great Dane, OD'd on speed, disappeared,
was found later in a mental hospital.

It has worked out in different ways.
Norman is in the High Sierra, killing his own deer.
The birds have been killed by a raccoon, who slit
their nylon cage, ate most of them. Imogene,
like a mafia *capo,* is taking over.

Nothing is as it was guaranteed to be.
She is not a Lhasa Apso, she is a Shih Tzu.
She has grandfathers and great-grandfathers, she has
her own number with the American Kennel Club.
She is in fact known, an aristocrat.

For the first three days I thought she was
timorous, elderly, a quiet dog
who would sit by the fireplace of evenings, who
could be taught to knit. After all these years
I should recognize, when I see it, shock.

I could and do recognize resilience.
Out of the wound of loss, of nobody,
it takes little to make her again feel
a person, to bark angrily, to say
"I am a person again. Let me in."

What were those weeks like, in the almost
unattended pet shop, where there was food
but nothing else? Svidrigailov says of eternity
"What if it were only a small bath-house
full of spiders?"

It is something, at least, to be in time
rather than in eternity. We may howl,
child, dog, at being bathed, tied up
while we dry. Yet it is a touch.
Why bark if you know there is no one listening?

So the aristocrats must have
crossed the Russian border to Shanghai,
knowing that they were nothing they had been before,
must have got jobs as *maîtres-d'hôtel,*
as cafe waitresses.

Must have come out of shock, into
a knowledge, tentative at first, that
it was possible to be human, must have said
to the world that was not their world "I have revised
my conceptions of being human. Let me in."

For many, there will have been those weeks
in the abandoned pet shop, when one was neither
owned nor believed in. There will have been
a break in the continuity of life.
"I was myself, or nothing. Nothing, then."

And as the Jews walked in their ritual order
to the chambers that would displace them, a space
opened in the middle of life, empty. Then
to one woman boarding the train, a neighbor
finally offered a sandwich.

A raccoon has eaten the birds, we do not
all survive, there is final and less than final.
Imogene will survive, she is fortunate.
I have given her a name other than her own name.
It is a device to change her luck.

And perhaps there is no place in her memory
to remember when she was nothing. If so, good.
She has now a plastic beetle that squeaks to play with.
She plays with it enthusiastically, wants other people
to play with her. It may be enough.

Sagittarius, Scorpio Rising

December monitors the known world, dismisses it.
Flat and frozen, the fields stretch
to a wee horizon, which the sun,
the size of a tangerine, bobs over
for an hour a day.
People are carved into the chalk of the hills,
their bodies lines.
Only the most antique, the most venerable.

O for a pregnant belly, for fat,
for a wastage of fat, an overflow
down the greasy channels beside the mouth,
circles bumping against one another
and getting bigger. Anything but this iron grid.

Sagittarius, in a fur hat, cold hands,
sits doing up his meticulous account
in a heavy leather journal. Although
subtracting diminishes what there is to have
there is some satisfaction in it.
At a predictable point in this long night
the idea of Zero will enter the zero room.

Looking ahead, Sagittarius can see
nothing but the worst.
If he sleeps, mostly he dreams of cars,
how they collide against one another without control,
how they lose traction on the snow hill,
how, when they are most needed, they will not make
the cold start.

Where is the land where lemons are in bloom?
Leopards pin butterflies to the ground with delicate paw,
release them, out of simple magnificence,
willingly accept collars of emeralds,
pad, unleashed, side by side
with naked muscular princes who are their friends.

Whatever that is, it is not arithmetic.
In worn leopard-skin boots up to the thighs,
a leopard-skin truss holding his loins together,
Sagittarius snuffs his candles and goes to bed
under blanket upon blanket upon blanket.

O for a fat sun! O for the break of weather!

Joy

It was all an appropriate if nervous afternoon,
explaining to a class of strange students the definition
of myself that I carry with myself to be exhibited.
The response was mixed. The hostile girl, in love
probably with the class's usual instructor
corrected me about Plato; the black girl laughed.
Then a man asked, unexpectedly, "Where do you find joy?"

Now I am driving my small car up the Coast Highway.
The motor is regular, the headlights are dipped and raised
to accommodate other travellers. I am warm and alone
between the dark vigorous sea and the dark mountains.
This is contentment, surely, but it is not joy.

Lying beside me, his arms behind his head
on the blue pillow, relaxed after making love,
my smooth, small lover said abruptly: "Are you happy?"
It had been a good day: we had eaten well,
making love was exciting; I admired his beauty.
But the question came out of nowhere and filled the room.

I go back years in time, to a summer morning
in the San Juan Islands, up before anyone else,
sitting on a rock over the beach in the early sunshine
watching the first ferry of the day make its calm passage
over the calm water, the wake unbroken behind it.

To a road between twenty-foot walls of snow, and a boy singing,
to a college room at dusk, the approach of Christmas,

and in the distance a choir of women's voices
singing, in Latin, how Christ is indeed born.

Is joy always in the past, the unnoticed turning
I have driven the car beyond because the car
has its own destiny, a place it is required to go,
and because time is linear and numerical and we move along it
like a function of it, no grace for its interruption?

The world fills with questions as a night sky fills,
using more space than had seemed available.
Space fills with the communication of the stars
experiencing joy, if I could speak their language,
great rhythms and sobs of fire.

Who was that young man, a messenger sent to ask me,
before the final day, for an accounting?
He did not stay for his answer. He may have left,
and walked out of the lecture room, unfurled his wings,
ascended with steady beat into the serene sky,
having induced the disquiet he was meant to bring.
He and his may peer down now, over the bowl's edge, smiling.

Small, in my small car, up the two-lane Coast Highway,
I drive, a middle-class man in his fifties, thinking,
flicking the high beam of the headlights up and down.
The day describes itself carefully in my mind.
The odometer keeps its accumulating measure.
Plenitude: the world contains everything that it can contain.
Nothing is left out, from the beginning of time.

In that completeness, where is the space for joy,
which must be, without a place singled in which to be,
startle into the heart without attitude or warning?
If I could find it I would, if I could believe
joy is so sensible as to be caught by finding.

Making Love

Making love the mirror watches
and imitates the white bodies
as it tries to learn.

All of the city is grouped
in attitudes of observance.
Its streets gravitate
to a growing center.
Everything tries: railway trains,
even the philosophical stars,
however unfitted.

This is to say how
dangerous making love is,
because to become aware of
one animate, intimate,
is to loosen the pictures on the walls
into noisy participation.

I thought it was only you.
How we would tighten ourselves into
a terse jewel.

Instead, over the house
helicopters gather and breathe raggedly.

Bread and its component parts
jitter in the night kitchen.

Being Asked to Define
Bourgeois Individuality

This poem is about being middle class.
It is about having time left over.

Kings have no time left over; they have
to kill their usurpers; peasants have
no time left over, they have to milk
cows that are endless, cows
that have to be milked
or they will spoil.

This is a poem about my sitting
in a house in St. John's Wood, London,
a house that has been loaned to me,
and thinking
what is it I most want to do
with this favorable day?

It is about Charles Darwin
getting up in the morning, thinking
a good day to begin
The Origin of Species.
Or a good day to go for a long country walk.

This poem thinks of a nineteenth-century world,
a bourgeois world: under the green glass lamp,
at evening, around the circular family table,
my daughters work at their sensitive water colors.

At morning, a table is laid for morning.
I have thought carefully about where to procure
the sausages. I have instructed the servants.

This is the world out of which,
as soon as morning is established as being morning,
I can escape.

Not kings escape, not Members of
Parliament, not judges
in their strange wigs. I escape
into that immense room, that immense meadow.

It is the place, the room, of available time.
I eat a time no other person has eaten.
Neither an animal nor a mineral even has eaten.

To the question, I say, this is
bourgeois individuality.
What we buy with our bodies and our lives
is time.

Cherish it.
Neither you nor I
will ever go to bed
with a better lover.

The Pruned Roses

If I had, uncut, the fingernails
and the toenails, all I have grown since birth,
I would be in a garden of hedges,
translucent loops, coils: Sleeping Beauty.
Topiary effects.

If I had all the hair I have ever grown
it would be a mediaeval river: hair
from here to the end of the night, growing
in bracelets, wristlets, amulets,
avocets, arguments. Rapunzel
has only herself to blame.

So much of us gets cut.
Flint knife, flint table of circumcision.
Baby howls at the blood. Young women, men,
hold themselves out eagerly to the cicatrices.
We recognize, in our flint notebook,
rite de passage.

Animals wear down, because they have to keep moving
what is unnecessary to their bodies:
hooves, antlers, otherwise it builds up.
Pony on ten-inch platform feet, stag
trapped in the interlocking of the spring branches.

Cut, wear, corrupt. Of course we will do that.
These notes are infirm, skeletal. They are meant
to inform pure essences who will come from space
and wonder what we meant by body. It was a thing
growing and cut back. The pruned roses.

The New Place

Already I begin, at morning
or at evening, not in the day's center, to live
slightly in the new place, which is not found,
but which is itself preparing, clearing its throat slightly,
telling its tenants how in a month,
two months, they will no longer be its
but another's, how there will no longer be
that intimacy that they have fallen into.

How many decisive ideas, founded on
security of place, will I now not ever achieve here.
They will remain
desolate for a while, asking for the
minds of the new inhabitants, who will not want them.
At morning, at evening,
dust rolls will drift from the place
where the argument was. All the rooms
down to the bare floors, stop experiencing my music.

Meanwhile the new place, wherever it is
concentrates on essentials. It will have
a few days, empty, to think
of what to assert, and then this stranger,
entering to the sound of fat trumpets, will walk
possessively across its floors. Its strength is in
the passivity of its doors and windows, how these must,
whatever else changes, remain structural.

As it looks out from its walls through the eyes
of pictures that have not before been its eyes,
there will be a hesitation of focus, a neutral time

before amity or enmity. The laying on of rugs
will begin to disguise it, but it is not
required of it willingly to accept the disguise.
A little wind blowing over the sill of a warped door—
it can express displeasure.
Make the view, if there is a view, occlude.

In order to make it think of me as desirable
I will take presents, the bridegroom
on his caparisoned horse, attended
by representatives of his mother's and father's families.

I will bring it gifts. Some things must be bought new.
New ideas are the resonating notes given off
by new possessions. The excitement of the new space.
That will be the food of this banquet of introductions.

Then I will put back the embroidered veils
from its unknown forehead, and we will be left
alone in each other's wilderness of language,
making and mocking our involvement with slow signs.
Love will be the outgrowth of amusement
at our own clumsiness, of the inevitable knowledge
that, living in each other's presence for how many years,
we will be, at morning and evening, those times
of departing from or entering the other dream,
no more than accidents, partial answers erased by time,
even as we seek our accommodation in one another.

Coyote's Song

How would it be, then, if I showed you
three shells and a pea under one of them,
and you guessed which one, and guessed right
and saved the world?

Good intentions never save the world, it takes tricks.

How would it be if I showed you all the gods
put together at one table, fat from eating
deermeat and bearmeat and salmon, unconcerned
about what happened to people, forgetting people?

They are good forgetters, that is what makes them gods.

I know you distrust me, you are so pure of heart,
and you think I will steal your tradegoods, or even
take away your children and rear them as my own.
Those are real fears on your part, I do not deny it.

The double mind knows what the single fears.

But it seems to me that you have no choice. Either
you put your trust in me, whom you cannot trust,
and I save you out of the pure pleasure of surprise,
or you doom yourselves to heroism and defeat.

Think of your children as being among your choices.

Painting with my brush of a tail, I make this plan:
it is a diagram of how to undo the gods;

it is a sacred diagram, involving laughter.
We laugh at the difference between two worlds.

I laughed at the gods, it is why I am disinherited.

I hide the children in a secure cave, I put clay children
in their place. The gods, who are single of vision
cannot tell the difference. They ask for sacrifices.
When there are none, they destroy the clay children.

The gods and the clay children pass together into myth.

Freed from the tyranny of the gods, you and your children
will inhabit the earth in richness and perplexity,
wondering whose was the trick, who was the trickster,
laughing because you are unsure what to believe.

It is my gift to you, it will make you human.